Thriving in Business

ESSENTIAL TRAINING FOR SAVVY ENTREPRENEURS

Sara Larson

BALD AND BONKERS
NETWORK
Academy

Bald and Bonkers Network Academy

First Printing, 2024

ISBN: 979-8-8691-9747-4
EISBN: 979-8-8691-9748-1

Thriving in Business

Disclaimer

This book has been crafted solely for informational purposes. Every endeavor has been undertaken to ensure its completeness and accuracy. Nevertheless, there might be inadvertent errors in typography or content. Furthermore, the information presented herein is accurate only up to the date of publication. Hence, this book should be utilized as a guiding tool rather than an absolute authority.

The objective of this book is to enlighten. The author and the publisher do not guarantee the absolute completeness of the information provided herein and disclaim any responsibility for errors or omissions. Neither the author nor the publisher shall be held liable or accountable to any individual or entity for any losses or damages, whether direct or indirect, purportedly arising from the use of this book.

This book serves as a resource for educational purposes exclusively. It is not intended to replace professional medical advice, diagnosis, or treatment. Therefore, reliance solely on this information is discouraged, and individuals are advised to seek professional medical guidance when necessary.

Contents

1

~

A Quick Introduction

You have embarked upon the captivating journey into the dynamic and ever-evolving realm of business—a voyage both exhilarating and formidable. In this world, where innovation intertwines with challenge, the pursuit of building and nurturing a thriving business transcends mere inspiration and industriousness. It necessitates the cultivation of a distinct mindset and the implementation of effective strategies capable of navigating the labyrinthine landscape of entrepreneurship.

Mindset and strategies stand as the twin pillars

upon which entrepreneurial triumph finds its footing. They are the guiding lights that ignite the flame of innovation, sustain the fire of determination, and empower entrepreneurs, such as yourself, to chart a course through the complex and perpetually shifting currents of the business world.

Whether you are a seasoned veteran seeking to hone your expertise or a budding visionary embarking on the uncharted waters of entrepreneurship, understanding and harnessing the power of mindset and strategic acumen will profoundly influence your journey toward success.

Why does mindset hold such paramount importance? The mindset of an entrepreneur serves as the crucible wherein their perspective is forged, their decisions are shaped, and their resilience is tested in the crucible of adversity. It forms the bedrock upon which businesses are erected, fostering creativity, adaptability, and an unyielding commitment to realizing one's objectives.

Consider, for instance, the transformative potential of a growth-oriented mindset. Entrepreneurs who embrace this mindset perceive challenges not as obstacles but as stepping stones to growth and development. They possess the resilience to rebound from setbacks with renewed determination, viewing failure not as a finality but as a springboard toward greater achievements.

Similarly, your strategies serve as the architectural blueprint for your journey to success. A well-crafted strategy is not merely a roadmap but a compass, guiding you through the twists and turns of the entrepreneurial landscape, effectively allocating resources, and seizing upon opportunities as they arise. It ensures that every decision and action aligns harmoniously with the overarching vision, imbuing your endeavors with purpose and direction.

Implementing effective strategies empowers you to leverage your strengths, mitigate risks, and optimize your potential for sustainable growth. It fosters a culture of innovation, agility, and calculated risk-taking, enabling you to navigate the turbulent waters of entrepreneurship with confidence and poise.

Indeed, success in entrepreneurship is not a matter of happenstance or luck but a culmination of deliberate choices, a resilient mindset, and well-executed strategies. But how does one acquire these essential skills? Let us embark upon a deeper exploration of this inquiry.

2

~~

Developing the Entrepreneurial Mindset

Embarking upon the enthralling journey into the dynamic realm of business is not a mere endeavor of having a brilliant idea or possessing a unique product—though undeniably, such attributes serve as commendable starting points. It is a profound exploration into the cultivation of a mindset that transcends the ordinary, a way of thinking and approaching challenges that distinguishes the successful entrepreneur from the rest.

In the tapestry of entrepreneurial success, myriad traits and characteristics intertwine, each contributing its unique thread to the fabric of achievement. These qualities are not merely inherent gifts bestowed upon a select few but are rather attributes that can be nurtured and developed to enhance one's likelihood of realizing their goals.

Understanding the Traits and Characteristics of Successful Entrepreneurs:

1. Passion and Vision: At the core of every successful venture lies an unwavering passion, an ardent enthusiasm that ignites determination and fuels commitment. Successful entrepreneurs possess a clear and compelling vision that serves as the beacon guiding their endeavors, empowering them to set audacious goals and navigate the turbulent waters of entrepreneurship with unwavering focus.

2. Resilience and Perseverance: The path of entrepreneurship is strewn with obstacles and setbacks, demanding a steadfast resilience and unwavering perseverance. Successful entrepreneurs embrace failures not as stumbling blocks but as stepping stones

to success, leveraging each setback as an opportunity for growth and learning. They possess the resilience to bounce back from adversity with renewed determination and adaptability.

3. Risk-Taking and Decision-Making: Entrepreneurs are adept at navigating the delicate balance between risk and reward, understanding that calculated risks are often the catalysts for extraordinary outcomes. Successful entrepreneurs possess a keen sense of judgment and the ability to make informed decisions swiftly, weighing the potential rewards against the inherent risks involved.

4. Innovative Thinking: Innovation lies at the heart of entrepreneurship, driving the creation of novel solutions to existing problems and the identification of untapped opportunities. Successful entrepreneurs possess a penchant for thinking outside the box, challenging the status quo, and envisioning possibilities where others see limitations. They constantly seek to disrupt industries, improve existing products or services, and meet unmet needs in the market.

5. Adaptability and Flexibility: The landscape of business is ever-evolving, marked by shifting market trends, evolving consumer preferences, and disruptive technological advancements. Successful entrepreneurs demonstrate a remarkable adaptability and flexibility, swiftly pivoting their strategies to respond to changing circumstances. They embrace change as an opportunity for growth and innovation, positioning themselves to thrive in dynamic environments.

6. Continuous Learning: Lifelong learning is the cornerstone of entrepreneurial success, fueled by an insatiable curiosity and an unyielding commitment to personal and professional growth. Successful entrepreneurs invest in expanding their knowledge base through diverse channels, including books, mentors, networking events, and industry conferences. By staying abreast of emerging trends and acquiring new skills, they gain a competitive edge and remain at the forefront of their respective industries.

7. Self-Confidence and Self-Belief: Belief in one-self is a non-negotiable prerequisite for entrepre-

neurial success, serving as the bedrock upon which audacious dreams are realized. Successful entrepreneurs exude self-confidence and possess an unwavering belief in their abilities, even in the face of skepticism or adversity. They trust their instincts, take calculated risks, and persevere through challenges with unwavering determination.

While some may inherently possess these traits and characteristics, they are not immutable qualities reserved for the chosen few. Rather, they can be cultivated and honed through intentional effort and dedication, enabling aspiring entrepreneurs to transcend perceived limitations and unlock their full potential.

Developing a Growth Mindset and Overcoming Limiting Beliefs:

The mindset you cultivate shapes not only your actions but also your outcomes. By fostering a growth mindset—a belief that abilities and intelligence can be developed through dedication and hard work—you pave the way for continuous growth and improvement.

Shift from a fixed mindset to a growth mindset by incorporating the word "yet" into your vocabulary. Embrace challenges as opportunities for growth, reinforcing the belief in your capacity to learn and evolve.

View every experience—whether success or failure—as a stepping stone on your journey of growth and learning. Engage in continuous self-improvement through diverse avenues such as reading, attending workshops, and networking events.

Embrace failure as a valuable learning experience rather than a reflection of your abilities. Analyze setbacks, extract lessons, and apply them to future endeavors, understanding that failure is an inevitable part of the entrepreneurial journey.

Identify and challenge limiting beliefs that hold you back from realizing your full potential. Replace negative self-talk with positive affirmations, reframing your mindset to focus on possibilities rather than limitations.

Utilize feedback from mentors, peers, and customers as a catalyst for growth and improvement. Surround yourself with a supportive community of like-minded individuals who share your aspirations and goals.

Strategies for Maintaining Motivation and Resilience:

Maintaining motivation and resilience is essential for navigating the highs and lows of the entrepreneurial journey. Set clear goals and create a compelling vision to provide direction and purpose to your endeavors.

Understand the underlying motivations driving your entrepreneurial pursuits, connecting with your "why" to sustain your commitment during challenging times.

Celebrate small victories along the way, fostering a sense of accomplishment and reinforcing a positive mindset. Take care of your physical and mental well-being through self-care activities such as exercise, proper nutrition, and relaxation.

Build a robust support network of mentors and peers who can offer guidance, inspiration, and encouragement during moments of uncertainty. Surround yourself with individuals who share your passion for growth and are committed to supporting your journey.

Remember, maintaining motivation, resilience, and a growth mindset is an ongoing process that requires consistent effort and self-care. By embracing these strategies and nurturing your entrepreneurial spirit, you empower yourself to overcome obstacles, seize opportunities, and achieve extraordinary success in the dynamic world of business.

3

~~

Mastering the Art of Decision Making

Navigating the intricacies of decision-making within the realms of limited information and uncertain outcomes is not merely a task; it is an art form, a skill set that demands mastery to navigate the labyrinthine pathways of entrepreneurship successfully. In the ever-evolving landscape of business, where ambiguity is rife and the consequences of decisions profound, the ability to make judicious choices amidst uncertainty becomes paramount, distinguishing the savvy entrepreneur from the rest.

Before delving into the decision-making process, it is imperative to lay a solid foundation by establishing clear criteria to guide evaluations. Identifying and prioritizing key factors that align with your business objectives fosters clarity of purpose and enables focused deliberation, even in the absence of comprehensive data.

Yet, in situations where information is scarce, diligence becomes imperative. Utilizing every available resource to gather pertinent data—tapping into networks, conducting exhaustive research, and seeking expert opinions—becomes indispensable. Moreover, discerning patterns and trends within the data, even amidst uncertainty, empowers entrepreneurs to make informed decisions.

However, the crux of effective decision-making lies not in the accumulation of data alone but in the astute evaluation of potential risks and uncertainties associated with each choice. Anticipating and assessing worst-case scenarios allows for the formulation of contingency plans, fostering a proactive approach that instills a sense of preparedness in the face of uncertainty.

In scenarios where information remains elusive, adopting a test-and-learn approach can prove invaluable. Embarking on small-scale experiments or prototypes enables entrepreneurs to glean real-time feedback and validate assumptions, thus facilitating iterative decision-making and continuous learning.

As entrepreneurs progress along their journey, intuition emerges as a formidable ally in decision-making. While data and analysis are indispensable, it is often intuition that guides one through dynamic environments, particularly when swift decisions are warranted. Trusting one's instincts, honed through accumulated experience and expertise, and integrating them with available information, becomes essential in making the most judicious decisions.

Understanding the delicate interplay between risk and reward is equally pivotal. Entrepreneurial decisions necessitate striking a delicate balance between potential risks and rewards, a task that demands discernment and foresight. Quantifying potential risks and rewards, considering both internal and external factors, provides invaluable insight into the potential outcomes of a decision.

However, risk tolerance varies among entrepreneurs and is influenced by myriad factors, including financial stability, industry dynamics, and personal goals. Understanding one's risk appetite and aligning decisions accordingly is imperative to ensuring congruence between actions and objectives.

Implementing robust risk management strategies further fortifies decision-making prowess. Conducting thorough risk assessments and engaging in tasks such as scenario analysis enable entrepreneurs to anticipate and mitigate potential risks, thus minimizing adverse impacts and bolstering resilience in the face of uncertainty.

Despite the wealth of information available, decision-making can often be fraught with challenges, leading to decision paralysis or analysis paralysis. To circumvent these obstacles, establishing clear decision-making criteria and realistic timelines is imperative. Breaking down complex decisions into manageable components and streamlining options enables entrepreneurs to navigate decision-making with clarity and purpose.

Moreover, decision-making is not merely a cognitive process but a skill that can be honed through practice and self-awareness. By embracing a mindset of continuous improvement and learning from past experiences, entrepreneurs can refine their instincts and liberate themselves from paralysis, thus making more effective choices that propel their ventures toward success.

4

~

Navigating Failure and Success

In the intricate journey of entrepreneurship, both failure and success emerge as steadfast companions, each wielding profound influence on the trajectory of one's endeavors. The manner in which one navigates failure, leveraging it as a stepping stone toward eventual success, assumes a pivotal role in fostering personal growth, resilience, and ultimately, sustainable achievement. Failure, far from being a deterrent or a mark of inadequacy, unveils itself as a profound teacher, imparting invaluable lessons and insights that serve as the bedrock for future triumphs.

Embracing a growth mindset is the cornerstone of transforming failure into an opportunity for learning and growth. Rather than interpreting setbacks as indictments of personal capability, they should be regarded as temporary setbacks, invitations to refine strategies, bolster resilience, and ultimately propel oneself toward heightened success. Embracing challenges and setbacks not as stumbling blocks, but as invaluable learning experiences, nurtures a spirit of resilience and fortitude, infusing every setback with the potential for growth.

Reflection upon failures emerges as a crucial component of the learning process. Analyzing the contributing factors behind each setback, identifying specific mistakes or weaknesses, and extracting actionable insights lay the groundwork for informed decision-making in the future. Failure, when viewed not as a personal defeat, but as constructive feedback, provides invaluable guidance for refining strategies, honing approaches, and cultivating a more resilient entrepreneurial mindset.

Upon gathering such knowledge, proactive utilization becomes imperative. Iterating and pivoting strategies, making necessary adjustments, experimenting with novel approaches, and adapting to evolving circumstances are essential endeavors. Embracing a flexible mindset that perceives change not as a hindrance, but as an opportunity for growth and innovation, paves the way for continued progress and eventual success.

Amidst failures, it is crucial to acknowledge and celebrate the small victories along the way. Recognizing incremental progress, irrespective of its magnitude, fosters a positive mindset, bolsters morale, and provides the necessary motivation and resilience to persevere through challenges.

Success, while undoubtedly exhilarating, presents its own unique set of challenges. Effectively managing success entails maintaining momentum, guarding against complacency, and continuously striving for growth and innovation.

Maintaining a growth mindset, even amidst success, is imperative. Success should not be viewed as a final destination, but rather as another milestone in the journey of growth and achievement.

Recognizing the perpetual room for improvement, embracing the ethos of continuous growth and learning, and remaining open to new possibilities are essential for sustaining success in the long term.

To combat complacency, setting ambitious goals becomes imperative. These goals should transcend comfort zones, challenging individuals to attain new milestones, pursue excellence, and continuously raise the bar for achievement. Establishing specific, measurable, and time-bound objectives serves as a roadmap for focused action and relentless pursuit of progress.

Cultivating a culture of continuous improvement within the business sphere is paramount. Encouraging employees to seek out opportunities for innovation and optimization, leveraging both internal and external feedback, and fostering an environment that values experimentation and learning are crucial for staying ahead of the curve and maintaining competitive advantage.

To ward off stagnation, actively seeking out new challenges that stretch one's capabilities is advisable.

Exploring new markets, developing innovative products or services, and undertaking projects that push the boundaries of personal expertise serve as catalysts for growth, innovation, and differentiation within the marketplace.

Celebrating successes is imperative for fostering a positive organizational culture and maintaining morale. However, it is essential to remain grounded in the face of success, guarding against inflated egos or a loss of perspective. Recognizing the efforts of team members, expressing gratitude to mentors and supporters, and attributing success to collective effort fosters humility, camaraderie, and a shared sense of purpose.

Developing a healthy relationship with both failure and success is indispensable for long-term growth and well-being. Embracing failure as a natural part of the journey, reframing setbacks as opportunities for growth and learning, and practicing self-compassion in their aftermath cultivates resilience, fortitude, and emotional well-being.

Learning from failures enhances one's capacity

to celebrate successes with gratitude and humility. Expressing appreciation towards those who contributed to success, acknowledging the role of external factors and serendipity, and recognizing the interconnectedness of individual achievement with broader societal and economic dynamics fosters humility, gratitude, and a sense of interconnectedness.

Maintaining humility in the face of success ensures a balanced perspective and guards against hubris or complacency. Recognizing that success is often the result of collective effort, external factors, and fortuitous circumstances fosters humility, gratitude, and a sense of responsibility towards others.

Both failure and success should be regarded not as endpoints, but as integral components of a continuous journey of growth and achievement. Striving for self-improvement, setting new goals, and embracing a mindset of lifelong learning, adaptability, and resilience perpetuates the journey towards entrepreneurial success.

Maintaining a balanced perspective on both failure and success is paramount. Understanding that failure does not define one's worth, and success does not guarantee perpetual triumph, cultivates resilience, adaptability, and emotional well-being. By fostering a healthy relationship with both failure and success, entrepreneurs can navigate the uncertainties of the entrepreneurial journey with grace, resilience, and unwavering determination.

5

~

Idea Generation and Validation

Establishing the bedrock of a successful business begins with the conception of a stellar idea. However, for entrepreneurs, the process of generating and validating ideas that are both innovative and commercially viable poses a significant challenge.

Discovering and substantiating business ideas

The initial stride toward formulating a business idea involves pinpointing a problem in need of resolution. Delve into market inefficiencies, unearth unmet needs, and scrutinize pain points prevalent in the market or gleaned from personal experiences. Engage in brainstorming sessions to conceptualize solutions that not only address these issues but also offer substantial value to prospective customers.

Once a problem and potential solutions have been identified, conduct thorough market research to ascertain the demand for your idea. Evaluate competitors, delineate target demographics, and scrutinize industry trends to gauge the feasibility of your concept. Utilize the insights garnered to refine your idea and ascertain its alignment with market needs.

Prior to investing substantial resources, it is imperative to validate your idea. Solicit feedback from prospective customers, industry experts, and mentors to refine your concept and identify potential obstacles. Employ prototypes, minimum viable products, and pilot programs to assess the feasibility of your idea and refine your strategy accordingly.

Consideration of financial viability is also paramount. Assess the costs associated with launching and sustaining your business, encompassing production, marketing, and operational expenses.

Determine revenue streams and projected profits to ensure the sustainability of your business model.

To carve a niche in a competitive market, your business idea must boast a unique value proposition that sets it apart from rivals. Identify the distinguishing features of your idea, be it innovative functionality, competitive pricing, or exemplary customer service.

Understanding market demand and competition

Effectively targeting the right audience and devising robust strategies concerning market demand and competition are indispensable for success.

Embarking on market research serves as the primary step in comprehending potential market demand and competitive landscape. Acquire insights into customer needs, preferences, and behaviors through demographic analysis, surveys, interviews, and focus groups. Uncover pain points, discern desires, and comprehend purchasing habits to tailor your offerings accordingly.

Thoroughly studying competitors is imperative.

Familiarize yourself with their strengths, weaknesses, and market position. Scrutinize their product offerings, pricing strategies, marketing endeavors, and customer feedback to discern market gaps and differentiate your offerings effectively.

Based on the amassed data, narrow down your target market. Define your ideal customer profile and formulate buyer personas to grasp their characteristics and preferences. This aids in product development tailored to their specific needs.

Evaluate the growth potential of your target market. Ascertain whether it is sizable enough to sustain your proposed business and explore opportunities for expansion. Delve into market trends, economic conditions, and industry forecasts to gauge the future viability of your target market.

Market demand and competition are dynamic entities. Continuously monitor market trends, gather customer feedback, and scrutinize competitor strategies. Stay abreast of industry developments, emerging technologies, and shifting customer preferences to adapt your offerings and strategies accordingly, thereby maintaining competitiveness and catering to evolving market demands.

Development and testing of a Minimum Viable Product (MVP)

The concept of a Minimum Viable Product (MVP) has emerged as a favored approach for entrepreneurs to test and validate their business ideas in a cost-effective and efficient manner.

To craft an MVP for your business, identify the core value or key features that your product or service will offer to alleviate the target market's problem. Determine the essential functionality that delivers the most significant value to users, prioritizing development efforts and maintaining focus.

With the core value established, develop a rudimentary prototype or a simplified version of your product or service showcasing this value. Whether a mock-up, wireframe, or basic functional version, the prototype serves as a tangible representation of your idea, facilitating testing and validation.

Engage a select group of early adopters or target customers willing to provide feedback. Share the MVP with them and observe their interactions and responses. Gather insights, suggestions, and pain points to refine the product further.

Iterate and refine your MVP based on received feedback. Address any identified shortcomings, usability issues, or areas for improvement, fostering alignment with customer needs and expectations. This iterative process ensures continual enhancement of your product to cater to evolving requirements.

During the testing phase, define key metrics aligned with your business objectives and monitor them closely. Track user engagement, conversion rates, customer satisfaction, or any other pertinent performance indicators. Analyzing these metrics facilitates the assessment of MVP effectiveness and informs data-driven decisions.

Leverage insights garnered from MVP testing to make informed decisions regarding further development or pivoting of your idea. Pivot if significant flaws or gaps are identified, and proceed if the feedback validates market demand. These testing phases elucidate whether your idea aligns with market demand, minimizing risks, maximizing learning, and empowering you to develop products that resonate with customer needs and expectations.

6

∿

Business Planning and Execution

Following the formulation of your meticulously crafted business plan with clearly delineated goals, you embark on a journey guided by strategic vision. These goals not only serve as beacons for your decision-making but also steer the allocation of resources, ensuring seamless alignment with the overarching vision of your enterprise.

Drafting a business plan and delineating goals

Your business plan must encapsulate your vision, mission, target demographic, value proposition, competitive analysis, marketing strategies, operational blueprints, and financial forecasts. Inclusive of a comprehensive description of your products or services, pricing strategy, distribution channels, and organizational structure, a meticulously crafted business plan not only charts the trajectory of your business but also serves as a pivotal tool for attracting investors and securing funding.

Inculcating SMART goals—Specific, Measurable, Achievable, Relevant, and Time-bound—into your business strategy is paramount. Segmenting long-term objectives into shorter-term milestones facilitates the creation of a lucid roadmap. Concurrently, the delineation of key performance indicators (KPIs) aids in gauging progress and achievements.

When endeavoring to attain your goals, partitioning them into more manageable components facilitates progress. Identifying critical activities and requisite resources for each goal, subsequently prioritizing these activities based on their potential impact, enables effective resource allocation, encompassing financial, human capital, and technological aspects.

Effective execution necessitates a fusion of strategic planning, flexibility, adaptability, and seamless teamwork, catalyzing the metamorphosis of your entrepreneurial aspirations into tangible reality.

Building a team and delegating responsibilities

To scale your business and concentrate on strategic imperatives, fostering a robust team is indispensable.

Thoroughly delineating roles and requisite skill sets imperative for realizing your business objectives is pivotal. Ponder over core competencies, expertise, and experiences essential for each role to assemble a team brimming with aptitude.

Pursuing top-tier talent mandates a rigorous recruitment strategy. Leveraging myriad channels such as job boards, professional networks, and referrals facilitates the identification of prospective candidates. Rigorous evaluation via applications and interviews discerns qualifications, cultural alignment, and resonance with your vision. Prioritize individuals poised to inject diverse perspectives and harbor a fervent passion for your industry.

Cultivating a work environment conducive to collaboration and open communication is imperative. Fostering a culture underpinned by trust, respect, and innovation fosters an ecosystem wherein team members proffer ideas, solicit feedback, and espouse the growth mindset integral to your odyssey.

Communication is a shared responsibility. It behooves you to ensure each team member comprehends their responsibilities and performance expectations, thereby catalyzing alignment with the overarching business objectives. Endowing them with clarity regarding goals, deadlines, and deliverables emboldens them to assume ownership of their tasks and synchronize their endeavors with the overarching vision.

Leveraging the capabilities and individual strengths of your burgeoning team to delegate tasks and responsibilities facilitates equitable workload distribution, factoring in each member's capacity. Empowerment through provision of requisite resources, authority, and autonomy propels them toward the successful execution of their designated responsibilities. Maintaining personal efficacy necessitates collaborative efforts, eschewing undue burden.

A cohesive and empowered team constitutes the linchpin for focusing on strategic initiatives, fostering innovation, and propelling your business forward.

Scaling and growing a business

Embarking on the trajectory of scaling and expanding your business is imbued with excitement, albeit contingent upon meticulous execution.

Articulating a growth strategy delineates objectives, target markets, and expansion plans. Ponder over opportunities for organic growth, encompassing entry into new geographical markets or diversification of product/service offerings. Strategic partnerships, acquisitions, or franchising serve as potential conduits for expansion.

Before embarking on the trajectory of scaling

your business, streamlining operations is imperative. Optimize processes, automate tasks where feasible, and invest in technology augmenting productivity while curtailing costs. Ongoing optimization facilitates accommodation of burgeoning demand and underpins scalability.

Team dynamics play a pivotal role in scaling endeavors. The recruitment and nurturing of talented individuals are pivotal catalysts for growth. Cultivating a robust leadership team empowers efficient management and alignment toward growth objectives.

Regular monitoring of KPIs and metrics facilitates tracking progress toward growth objectives. Periodic assessment of strategy effectiveness engenders data-driven adjustments, fostering agility and adaptability commensurate with market dynamics and customer needs.

Embarking on the pursuit of new target markets necessitates a revisit to market research endeavors. Comprehensive comprehension of emerging needs, preferences, and purchasing behaviors underpins successful expansion efforts.

Nurturing a robust brand constitutes a quintessential investment. Ensure resonance with your target audience by developing a compelling value proposition, communicating unique selling propositions, and consistently delivering superlative customer experiences. Elevate brand awareness via effective marketing modalities such as social media, public relations, and customer engagement, thereby ensuring brand salience amid market dynamics.

7

~~

Marketing and Sales

The bedrock of successful marketing and sales strategies rests upon a profound comprehension of your target audience and their exigencies. By delving into their preferences, motivations, and pain points, entrepreneurs can tailor their offerings and devise efficacious communication strategies.

Comprehending your target audience and customer needs

Once again, meticulous market research assumes paramount importance here, leveraging insights gleaned into your target audience. Analyzing demographic data, psychographic characteristics, and purchasing behaviors is imperative. Understand the preferences, challenges, and aspirations of your audience through surveys, interviews, and focus groups, amalgamating qualitative and quantitative data to sculpt effective marketing and sales strategies.

Crafting fictional profiles, or buyer personas, incorporating demographic information, motivations, goals, pain points, and buying patterns humanizes your audience. This exercise facilitates personalized marketing messages resonating with their specific needs and desires. For instance, envisioning a buyer persona like Brian, a 37-year-old married man with two children, working full-time after earning his bachelor's degree in marketing, provides insights into his preferences and habits, enriching your marketing endeavors.

These buyer personas metamorphose your target audience from mere data points into relatable individuals. By discerning their needs, challenges, and pain points on a human level, you can position your offerings as solutions that proffer value and alleviate their struggles.

Developing a brand and messaging strategy

Your brand and messaging serve as the differentiating factor from competitors. A well-defined brand identity and compelling messaging foster brand awareness, engender trust with customers, and articulate the unique value of your products or services.

To craft this strategy, delineate your brand's core values, mission, and vision, elucidating what sets your business apart from competitors. Identify the key attributes defining your brand's personality, encompassing brand voice, tone, and visual elements like logos, colors, and fonts.

Subsequent to conducting market research into your target audience and crafting buyer personas, crafting the brand and voice of your company becomes more streamlined. Your value proposition, contingent upon this vital information, must communicate the unique benefits and value your brand offers, concisely differentiating you from competitors.

Constructing a poignant brand narrative that resonates with customers emotionally is pivotal. Share the journey behind your business, your mission, and the impact you aspire to create, fostering an authentic connection with your audience while setting your brand apart.

While employing myriad marketing channels, consistency in brand messaging and touchpoints is paramount. Whether on your website, social media platforms, advertising campaigns, or customer interactions, maintain a uniform tone, voice, and visual identity to fortify brand recognition and foster trust among your audience.

The objective is to cultivate relationships with customers through personalized and meaningful interactions. Nurturing brand loyalty entails furnishing exceptional customer experiences and consistently delivering on your brand promise. Encourage customer feedback and address their needs to fortify their bond with your brand.

As your business burgeons and market dynamics shift, your brand and messaging strategy may necessitate adjustments. Stay attuned to market trends, heed customer feedback, and remain ahead of competitors, perpetually evaluating and adapting your messaging to align with evolving customer needs and preferences.

Building and executing a sales plan

To drive revenue, acquire customers, and attain sales targets, a well-defined sales plan is indispensable, delineating strategies, tactics, and actions requisite for efficaciously selling products or services.

Initiate by setting clear and measurable sales goals and objectives, defining revenue targets, customer acquisition goals, and other key performance indicators aligning with predetermined business objectives. This provides a clear direction for your sales endeavors.

Devise strategies and tactics to realize your sales goals, discerning the most effective sales channels and approaches based on your target audience, market research, and buyer profiles. Create a comprehensive sales playbook outlining steps, processes, and techniques for your sales team to adhere to.

Building a proficient and motivated sales team is paramount. Recruit individuals aligned with your company culture, possessing robust communication and relationship-building skills, as they will be the vanguards in communicating directly with your customers.

Efficient sales processes underpin sustained success. Streamlining your sales cycle and leveraging customer relationship management (CRM) software to track leads, manage customer interactions, and monitor sales activities is indispensable. Implementing sales automation tools augments productivity and streamlines administrative tasks.

A well-executed sales plan necessitates continuous evaluation, adaptation, and a customer-centric approach to effectively meet market demands and drive sales success.

8

～

Giving Back and Making a Difference

Utilizing business as a vehicle for effecting change transcends mere profitability and success. It entails fostering a positive impact on society and the environment. By integrating social and environmental responsibility into their business practices, entrepreneurs seize the opportunity to give back and make a meaningful difference.

Using business as a force for good

Once the purposes and core values of your business are defined, identifying social and environmental issues that resonate with your values and align with your industry becomes paramount. This alignment guides your endeavors in giving back and creating a meaningful impact.

Adopting sustainable business practices can mitigate your environmental footprint. This encompasses initiatives such as waste reduction, energy conservation, utilization of eco-friendly materials, and implementation of recycling programs. By prioritizing sustainability, you contribute to a healthier planet and inspire others to do the same.

Ensure that your supply chain adheres to ethical and responsible practices. Forge partnerships with suppliers and vendors who share your commitment to fair labor, human rights, and environmental sustainability. By championing ethical supply chains, you contribute to a global ecosystem that upholds respect for both people and the planet.

Foster a positive and inclusive work environment

that values and supports your employees. Provide opportunities for personal and professional development, advocate for work-life balance, and institute fair and ethical labor practices. Empowered employees become ambassadors for your brand's positive impact.

Incorporating social responsibility into business strategy

Developing a comprehensive Corporate Social Responsibility (CSR) strategy that aligns with your values and addresses social issues is imperative. This may involve supporting local communities, donating a portion of profits to charitable causes, or volunteering time and resources. Collaborate with nonprofit organizations or initiate your own programs to effect positive change.

Set goals for your social responsibility initiatives, defining desired outcomes and specific actions required to achieve them. Incorporate these objectives into your day-to-day operations, considering ethical sourcing and supply chain practices, waste reduction, environmental impact mitigation, diversity and inclusion promotion within your workforce, and prioritization of fair and responsible labor practices. Integrate these principles into your policies, procedures, and decision-making processes.

Engage stakeholders, including employees, customers, suppliers, and the local community, in your social responsibility efforts. Communicate your goals, initiatives, and progress transparently. Encourage feedback and collaboration to ensure that your actions align with the expectations and needs of all stakeholders.

Building a legacy beyond financial success

While financial success often constitutes a primary goal, establishing a lasting legacy transcends monetary achievements. It entails making a meaningful and enduring impact on the world, leaving a positive imprint on people's lives. A legacy encompasses the values, principles, and contributions that endure long after the business journey concludes.

Begin by defining your purpose and values, identifying what truly matters beyond financial gains.

Recognize the principles and beliefs guiding your actions and decision-making. This clarity shapes the legacy you aspire to leave behind.

Cultivating positive relationships is pivotal. Invest in building robust relationships with stakeholders, including employees, customers, partners, and the community. Foster a culture of trust, respect, and collaboration. Leave a lasting impression through integrity, empathy, and genuine care for others.

Take the time to mentor and inspire others, especially new entrepreneurs or individuals within your industry. Share knowledge, experiences, and lessons learned. Encourage and empower others to pursue their dreams and make a difference in their own lives and communities.

Foster a culture of continuous learning and growth within your organization. Encourage employees to develop their skills, pursue passions, and realize their full potential. Invest in their professional and personal development. By nurturing a learning environment, you leave a legacy of empowered and fulfilled individuals.

Consider documenting your entrepreneurial journey and sharing your story. Capture the challenges, triumphs, and lessons learned along the way. Share insights through books, articles, speaking engagements, or digital platforms. Inspire others with experiences and provide a roadmap for them to follow.

Your legacy is the imprint you leave on people's lives and the positive change you bring to the world.

9

~~

Entrepreneurial Mindset for Life

The entrepreneurial mindset transcends the realm of business ventures alone; it constitutes a potent approach applicable to all facets of life. By embracing the entrepreneurial mindset, individuals can nurture personal and professional growth, seize opportunities, and surmount challenges.

Applying the entrepreneurial mindset to personal and professional growth

Embracing this mindset enables individuals to navigate challenges, embrace opportunities, and continually evolve in all spheres of life. The growth mindset fosters the belief that abilities and skills can be cultivated through dedication and effort. It encourages viewing challenges as opportunities for learning and improvement, not only in business but also in life at large. By maintaining a growth mindset, one remains receptive to new experiences and consistently seeks self-improvement.

Setting clear goals, specifically SMART goals, proves beneficial in personal life endeavors. Breaking down goals into specific, measurable, achievable, relevant, and time-bound categories provides a structured approach to addressing any problem or situation. This focused approach propels individuals towards growth and accomplishment.

The entrepreneurial mindset encourages stepping outside one's comfort zone, embracing new adventures while acknowledging that the fear of failure can hinder progress. Failures are perceived as pathways for growth and new opportunities. Taking risks facilitates the discovery of new paths, broadens horizons, and unlocks potential.

Resilience and adaptability hold equal significance. Cultivating resilience entails bouncing back from setbacks, learning from failures, and remaining committed to goals despite obstacles. Adaptability ensures thriving in our ever-changing world, enabling readiness to seize new opportunities as they arise.

Entrepreneurs thrive on creativity and innovation. Fostering creativity involves seeking new perspectives, exploring diverse interests, and embracing curiosity. Innovation entails finding unique solutions to challenges and continually seeking improvement in life.

Developing a lifelong learning strategy

Lifelong learning serves as the cornerstone of personal and professional growth, enabling individuals to adapt to a rapidly evolving world and stay ahead in their fields and lives. Cultivating a lifelong learning mindset necessitates developing a strategic approach that maximizes the benefits of continuous learning.

Begin by clarifying learning objectives, identifying the knowledge, skills, and expertise to be gained or enhanced, considering both personal and professional domains. Setting specific learning goals provides direction and motivation for the lifelong learning journey.

Explore available learning resources, encompassing books, online courses, workshops, conferences, webinars, podcasts, and mentoring programs. A combination of formal and informal learning opportunities enriches the knowledge base.

Commit to a regular learning schedule, allocating dedicated time each week or month for learning activities. Consistency is pivotal in building momentum and ingraining continuous learning as a habit.

Reflect on the learning journey, assessing progress, strengths, and areas for improvement. Self-reflection aids in tracking growth and identifying areas necessitating further development. Feedback from mentors or self-evaluation tools provides valuable insights into learning effectiveness.

Surround oneself with like-minded individuals on lifelong learning journeys, engaging in forums or social media groups. Networking within one's field fosters new learning opportunities and mentorships.

Apply newfound knowledge and skills in practical settings through projects, volunteering, or professional engagements. Sharing knowledge with others, through teaching or mentoring, solidifies understanding and contributes to the learning community.

Maintain curiosity, viewing lifelong learning as a continuous process. Adaptability and willingness to adjust learning goals ensure relevance in a changing world.

Navigating career transitions and new opportunities

Career transitions and new opportunities present a blend of excitement and challenge. Whether changing industries, pursuing a promotion, or exploring a different path, navigating these transitions demands careful planning and adaptability.

Reflect on skills, strengths, passions, and values, assessing alignment with desired career transitions or opportunities. Self-assessment forms a solid foundation for informed decisions and goal setting.

Thoroughly research the industry, role, or opportunity under consideration, including job market trends, required skills, and potential challenges. Seek insights and advice from professionals in the field and gain practical experience through internships or volunteering.

Identify potential skill gaps and proactively bridge them through courses, certifications, or workshops. Highlight transferable personal skills, emphasizing their value in the new context to combat imposter syndrome.

Seek professional mentors who have navigated similar transitions successfully, leveraging their insights and support to overcome obstacles.

The entrepreneurial mindset, characterized by resilience and persistence, equips individuals to embrace opportunities, particularly when coupled with a commitment to lifelong learning. Each transition presents opportunities for growth, learning, and personal fulfillment.

10

~

Conclusion

In the intricate tapestry of entrepreneurship, the threads of success intertwine with a delicate balance of mindset and strategic acumen. As we draw the curtains on this exploration, we unveil a mosaic of insights essential to the triumph of entrepreneurial endeavors. From the cultivation of a resilient mindset to the orchestration of meticulous strategies, each facet contributes to the fabric of success, weaving a narrative of growth, resilience, and opportunity. By weaving these diverse strands together, aspiring entrepreneurs can craft a framework poised for ascension, adeptly navigating the labyrinthine pathways of challenge and opportunity with unwavering resolve and confidence.

Harmonizing the Elements:

At the heart of entrepreneurial success lies the entrepreneurial mindset—a paradigm characterized by resilience, adaptability, and an insatiable thirst for growth. This mindset transcends the confines of business, permeating into the realms of personal development and fostering a holistic ethos of lifelong learning and advancement.

The efficacy of this mindset is inextricably intertwined with the implementation of strategic initiatives. From the inception of innovative ideas to the meticulous execution of business plans, each phase of the entrepreneurial journey demands meticulous planning, unwavering determination, and an astute understanding of market dynamics. By discerning market demand, validating ideas, and fortifying their positions in the competitive landscape, entrepreneurs can forge a path towards sustainable growth and scalability.

Central to the entrepreneurial narrative is the narrative of marketing and sales—the conduits through which entrepreneurs connect with their target audience and fulfill the needs of their customers. Crafting a compelling brand identity, honing persuasive messaging, and executing robust sales strategies are the cornerstones of a thriving enterprise. By infusing these strategies with a sense of social responsibility and community engagement, entrepreneurs not only propel their brands forward but also cultivate a legacy of positive impact and societal contribution.

Amidst the ebbs and flows of entrepreneurial endeavors, navigating the turbulent waters of failure and success emerges as a defining chapter in the narrative of triumph. Embracing failure as a crucible of growth and learning, entrepreneurs glean invaluable insights that propel them towards eventual success. Conversely, managing success demands a delicate balance of humility and confidence, ensuring that complacency does not stifle innovation, and momentum is maintained on the trajectory of growth.

Adaptability and agility emerge as indispensable attributes in the entrepreneurial arsenal, enabling entrepreneurs to pivot swiftly in response to evolving market dynamics and emerging opportunities. Navigating career transitions and exploring new avenues demand introspection, skill enhancement, and the cultivation of a robust professional network. Lifelong learning, underpinned by the growth mindset, empowers individuals to thrive amidst the ever-evolving currents of change, equipping them with the tools necessary to navigate uncharted territories with confidence and poise.

The Multifaceted Odyssey:

Success as an entrepreneur is not merely a destination but rather an ongoing odyssey—a voyage characterized by perpetual growth, learning, and evolution. By synthesizing the principles of mindset and strategy delineated herein, entrepreneurs can embark on a transformative journey of self-discovery and enterprise, charting a course towards enduring success and profound impact.

The entrepreneurial voyage, replete with its

trials and triumphs, calls forth an unwavering commitment to personal advancement, a readiness to embrace risk, and a steadfast belief in the transformative power of resilience and determination. By assimilating the insights garnered from this discourse, aspiring entrepreneurs can embark on a gratifying odyssey—a journey defined by resilience, innovation, and an unyielding dedication to leaving an indelible mark on both personal and collective spheres.